WHY YOU CAN'T PAY ATTENTION

HOW TO IMPROVE PRODUCTIVITY

AVIRAL PATHAK

Copyright © Aviral Pathak
All Rights Reserved.

TO SIR RATAN TATA

THE PERSON WHO INSPIRE NOT ONLY TO ME BUT TO EACH AND EVERY PERSON OF INIDA THANKS SIR TO MOTIVATE ME

Contents

Preface

Do you ever feel as if you can't sit down and work? Is your mind wandering constantly from one thought to another? Well, you're not alone.

Before moving on, I'll give you the solution upfront.

To stop procrastinating, you must eliminate all distractions from your life. As a result, your mind's focus capability- will increase.

Currently, many people scroll on social media for most of their days. Hence they habituate jumping from one piece of information to another.

Thus when they sit down to work, the value of their outcomes- will be inferior than if they had the capability of aiming their undivided attention toward a single goal.

Now, let's get started

ONE

DISTRACTIONS — THE KILLER OF PRODUCTIVITY

Statistics for the US report Instagram as the third-most-downloaded app with 62 million. TikTok and Zoom were first and second with 89 million and 81 million downloads, respectively.

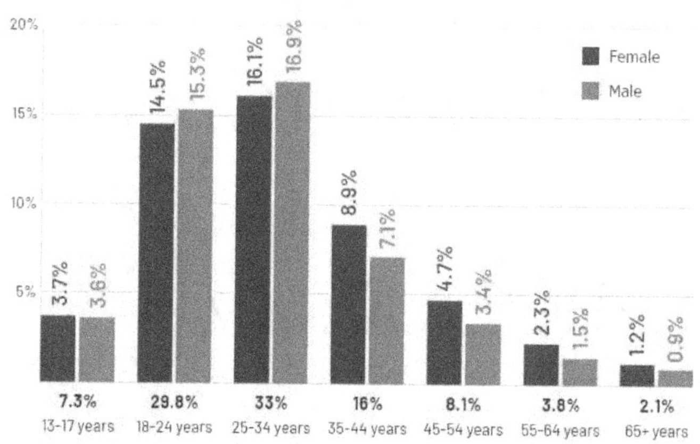

Data source

89 million people have downloaded Tiktok at some point in their lives. Do you see why it's a problem? If you don't, try and think about the time wasted on instant gratification instead of creating and being productive.

Countless go down the drain every single day. Additionally, you may also be a part of the group that favors consuming more than creating.

So, which group do you want to be a part of?

Few are the people who are capable of working on a single task for extended periods without getting distracted.

In fact, most people I know- have stopped trying to improve that pillar in themselves. They've given up hope on the matter of productivity.

Nonetheless, you may also turn your head into cheap entertainment when bored. Hence your attention span is lower than what it would've been if you started to focus

Why you don't want to work.

You have habitually jumped from one task to another by using social media. So, how does it work?

When scrolling on social media, your mind seeks the next dopamine hit. It'll do anything to feel that rush again.

Then, when you sit down to work, do you think your mind will be capable of focusing or rather aiming its undivided attention towards working, a low-stimulus action?

No way.

You don't want to work because your mind is looking for the next dopamine hit. But, like drug addicts, we can't live without our phones.

SO THE MAIN VILLAIN IS <u>DOPAMINE</u>

What Is Dopamine?

Dopamine is a type of neurotransmitter. Your body makes it, and your nervous system uses it to send messages between nerve cells. That's why it's sometimes called a chemical messenger.

Dopamine plays a role in how we feel pleasure. It's a big part of our unique human ability to think and plan. It helps us strive, focus, and find things interesting.

Your body spreads it along four major pathways in the brain. Like most other systems in the body, you don't notice it (or maybe even know about it) until there's a problem.

Too much or too little of it can lead to a vast range of health issues. Some are serious, like Parkinson's disease. Others are much less dire.

ok to be in a very simple manner

Dopamine is a neurotransmitter in our brains that motivates us to do activities that make us feel pleasure. When you engage in a pleasurable activity, dopamine releases in your brain.Pleasurable activities include simple things like eating, drinking, watching your favorite movie, listening to music, to "artificial" stimuli like playing video games, binge-watching Netflix, or gambling.

Too much dopamine, however, can lead to addiction, including drug addiction and video game addiction.

The more video games you play, the more you can need to play them to satisfy your needs, leading to disordered play or addiction.

In recent years, a new solution suggested by mental health specialists is a dopamine detox. Dopamine detox, or dopamine fasting, is a term first coined by <u>Dr. Cameron Sepah</u>, a Harvard psychiatrist from California.

Dopamine is a type of neurotransmitter. Your body makes it, and your nervous system uses it to send messages between nerve cells. That's why it's sometimes called a chemical messenger.

Dopamine plays a role in how we feel pleasure. It's a big part of our unique human ability to think and plan. It helps us strive, focus, and find things interesting.

Your body spreads it along four major pathways in the brain. Like most other systems in the body, you don't notice it (or maybe even know about it) until there's a problem.

Too much or too little of it can lead to a vast range of health issues. Some are serious, like Parkinson's disease. Others are much less dire.

ok to be in a very simple manner

Dopamine is a neurotransmitter in our brains that motivates us to do activities that make us feel pleasure.

When you engage in a pleasurable activity, dopamine releases in your brain.Pleasurable activities include simple things like eating, drinking, watching your favorite movie, listening to music, to "artificial" stimuli like playing video games, binge-watching Netflix, or gambling.

Too much dopamine, however, can lead to addiction, including drug addiction and video game addiction.

The more video games you play, the more you can need to play them to satisfy your needs, leading to disordered play or addiction.

In recent years, a new solution suggested by mental health specialists is a dopamine detox. Dopamine detox, or dopamine fasting, is a term first coined by <u>Dr. Cameron Sepah</u>, a Harvard psychiatrist from California.

What is the Dopamine Theory of Addiction?

The dopamine theory of addiction suggests an imbalance in dopamine production in the brain causes addictions.

Instead of getting enough dopamine from everyday activities, individuals suffering from addiction rely on receiving dopamine from drugs, alcohol, video games, or other external stimuli instead.

The addicted individual requires more of their stimuli of choice (drugs, alcohol, video games) to feel satisfied.

According to Mellis et al. (2005), the dopamine theory of addiction goes like this:

"Decreased DA (dopamine) function in addicted subjects results in a decreased interest to non-drug-related stimuli and increased sensitivity to the drug of choice."

The dopamine theory of addiction suggests that dopamine is at the center of the addiction. With research suggesting that dopamine is the driver behind addictive actions, professionals have started treating addictions by addressing dopamine.

What Triggers Dopamine?

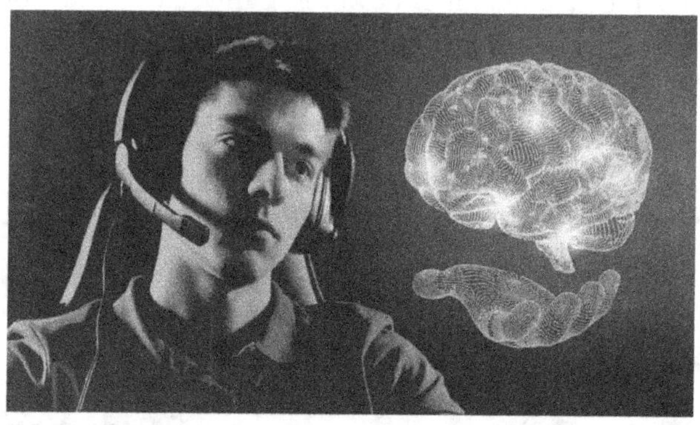

Dopamine is triggered by any pleasurable or rewarding activity we do. This includes everyday activities like eating or drinking to more addictive activities like taking drugs, alcohol, sex, or playing video games.

The key difference here is that some activities release more dopamine than others.

Taking drugs and playing video games produce an instant rush of dopamine. According to some studies, video games release large amounts of dopamine in our brains – comparable to when taking drugs like amphetamine. And because these activities release more dopamine than others, we feel more pleasure doing them. So, consequently, we do more of these activities.

Our brain gets used to the stimulus after some time, which means that we'll need to take more and more of the drug or play more video games to satisfy our needs. Other activities start to feel less enjoyable compared to our desired stimulus.

In addition, playing video games is convenient and sedentary, and it doesn't take much effort to experience pleasure. You only need to open your phone or computer and start playing the game, and you'll almost instantly begin experiencing stimulation and pleasure.

If we compare gaming to less convenient or higher effort activities that produce dopamine like going to the gym, playing video games starts to feel more comfortable. We can justify neglecting other activities for the instant gratification of gaming.

What are the Side Effects of Too Much Dopamine?

Dopamine is one of the most important chemicals in our brain. Its presence is required for normal functioning and often affects our mood and how we feel.

Having optimal amounts of dopamine is crucial for the normal functioning of our body, and it also helps us feel satisfied. Optimal levels of dopamine can contribute to being more alert, satisfied, productive, and motivated.

Having too much or too little dopamine can drastically change the way we live and feel.

The side effects of too much dopamine include:

ADHD

Addictions

Binge-eating and other binging behaviors

Gambling

Obesity

TWO
HOW TO DO A DOPAMINE DETOX – STEP BY STEP

So now that you know dopamine detoxes do work, how do you proceed from here?

We've prepared a step-by-step plan on how to do a dopamine detox properly.

Step 1: Decide to do Dopamine Detox and Commit to It

The first step begins with your mindset. Make sure your mindset is one where you believe in this process and believe in yourself to be successful with it.

But you must know that starting a dopamine detox takes time and dedication. You need to know it will get tough along the way, but you MUST be willing to stick to it. It's the only way.

Think about your current situation if you're addicted to video games. Do you want to continue like this? No motivation or energy to do anything else but to play video games all day?

Take a moment to think about why you want to quit playing video games. Then, imagine the life you want to live without your addiction. Then, please write it down and remember it. Writing out how you want to feel, your goals, and what you dream for your life will help keep you going when things get tough.

The detox is only going to work if you commit to it 100%. No "just one game" or "just one scroll of my Instagram feed."

Step 2: Delete Your Games and Accounts

Now that you've decided to stick to the dopamine detox, it's time to delete your games from your computer—all of them.

It might even be helpful to delete the accounts for the games you play most. If you have a lot of stuff on your account and you don't want to delete it, one option is to sell it.

The reason why deleting your games and accounts is effective is that after you've deleted them, you won't be able to jump into the game instantly.

You'll have to re-install the game, which can be too much of a bother for some people. But deleting your account will be even more effective since it might take you longer to create an account, so you might refrain from doing it altogether.

If you don't know how to delete your game accounts, we've created a series of helpful tutorials on Game Quitters that you can check out, showing you how to delete your accounts for various platforms.

Step 3: Start the Detox

Then it's time to start the detox.

Mark the happy day on your calendar and observe the changes that it brings to your life.

Step 4: Stick to It for 90 Days

Now you need to stick to it for 90 days.

Why 90 days?

Because research suggests, that's how long it may take for changes in your brain caused by addiction to begin reversing.

You might start experiencing some withdrawal symptoms, which is when it's good to remind yourself why you started the detox in the first place. It is also a good time to develop new coping strategies and learn how to navigate challenges in your life without escaping into games.

Also, you'll want to find replacement activities that will help you replace your gaming habit. Use our hobby tool to find a hobby that you like and try it. If you don't like it, you can always try another hobby.

Step 5: Continue or Stop

After 90 days, you should be feeling better with your cravings and urges to play significantly reduced.

You now have two options:

You can continue the detox and living a life without your gaming addiction.

Or, you can start playing games in moderation, as long as you have other things going on in your life.

If you don't know if you can't play in moderation, then it's up to you to try it. But it's better to be cautious if you're not sure, so you don't get drawn into an addiction cycle again.

here are my some friends review after applying this steps

"Having goals and watching yourself achieve them is the most satisfying feeling in the world. I don't even think about gaming anymore."

– rahul.m

"Since I gave up video games I have started to learn python and begun a yoga practice."

– atharva

"I reached 90 days and it's the longest I've gone without playing video games my entire life."

– sk gammer(now he is not gammer)hehehe.

"Yesterday I finished my 90 days!!! The first week was hard but worth it!!"

-its me yes (aviral) i have to apply on myself too

THREE
HOW TO IMPROVE PRODUCTIVITY

Productivity is a common measure of how well we're doing in each of those areas and relates to how efficiently a team is operating. Like most areas of leadership, productivity increases when an improvement on your team begins with your improvement as an individual.

We'll look at six strategic ways to help your team be more productive in the workplace, followed by an additional seven simple but effective ways to increase your personal productivity at work.

How to increase the team's productivity at work
<u>this steps can use by student and jobperson</u>

1. Set realistic goals

Here we are talking about goals again! Really, we can't emphasize this enough. You, your team, your whole company you all need good team goals that are understandable and attainable. Lack of well-defined goals and measures is a major contributor to project failure, accounting for 37% of failed projects according to one Project Management Institute survey.

Good goals are realistic, clear, and measurable. You can assess whether your goals are good by asking the following questions:

Can we accomplish this goal with the time, resources, and project management skills we currently have? (Is it realistic?)

Do we know exactly what is being asked of us? (Is it clear?)

Are there quantifiable indicators with which we can judge our success around each goal? (Is it measurable?)

The goals you set for your team will be different from your individual goals of course. (You have mad individual goals, right?) During the project plan, don't forget to get your team's input on what their goals should be as a group and as individuals.

2. *Monitor progress*

When you plan your project, you establish key performance indicators (KPIs) in the form of,

    budgets

    project timelines and

    quality expectations.

During the course of your project, you should regularly check your KPIs and keep track of project progress so you can catch issues and make corrections quickly. Having good reporting tools greatly increases the accuracy and ease of monitoring. Don't forget to celebrate successes when your KPIs tell you the team has achieved a goal.

3. Hold standing meetings

We already mentioned that you should avoid unnecessary meetings. When you really do need to have a group of people together to discuss something, consider making it a standing meeting. Sometimes called 'standups', a standing meeting is exactly what it sounds like: a meeting where everyone is standing.

The benefit of a standing meeting is that it reduces the tendency to waste time. If everyone is settled around a conference table, you're more prone to chit-chat and to run off on tangents. In a standing meeting, everyone has the sense that the meeting is meant to be brief (it is), and they'll stick to the subject at hand.

4. Create a healthy work environment

A positive work environment contributes to productivity in multiple ways such as the Pomodoro technique all of which contribute to increased productivity. When your team members are happy, they're more likely to think creatively, take calculated risks, support their coworkers, and stay organized at work longer.

You can also have some productivity games to plan within teams that help to align them together.

5. Give your team the right tools

No matter how happy, committed, or skilled your team members are, they can benefit from having good tools at their disposal. The project management tool has come a long way in the past several years, and you should take advantage of it. The best project management software has kanban boards and built-in collaboration tools that can keep you organized and boost efficiency.

6. Share these tips with your team

Why keep good information to yourself? Educate your team by sharing the above productivity tips with them. Maybe gamify your team's productivity at work by having a doodling contest during breaks or seeing who can go the longest without checking his phone.

Now that you've learned how to ramp up your team's productivity as well, let's discuss how to be more productive at work as an individual as well.

How to increase productivity at work as an individual

1. Learn to prioritize

Most people end up as project managers because they are good at getting things done. Then you become a project manager and are suddenly expected to get more things done in the same amount of time. How do you decide what to tackle first? One simple tool for prioritizing is the Eisenhower Matrix.

Also known as the Urgent-Important Matrix, this method helps you prioritize tasks based on their levels of urgency and importance. Tasks fall into one of four categories:

Urgent and important

Not urgent, but important

Not important, but urgent

Not urgent and not important

It's helpful to visualize your Eisenhower Matrix by drawing a simple chart. Make the Eisenhower Matrix a regular part of your routine, and commit to following through and the insights your gain.

2. Schedule your day strategically

Some people arrive at the office full of energy, and some of us need an hour and a cup of coffee before our brains are fully operational. Take note of when you're most productive at work, and schedule the most difficult tasks for those times.

If the post-lunch slump always gets you, use that time to check emails or pop into a coworker's office to touch base (only make sure you don't interrupt her most productive time in the process!).

3. Delegate

One of the biggest challenges of project management is realizing that you cannot do it all. You may have been made project manager because you're really good at getting things done.

That's great! But now there are many more things for which you're responsible. If tasks are piling up, access which ones must be done by you and delegate tasks that can be passed to someone else.

4. Reduce distractions

We live in a distraction-filled world, and whether we realize it or not, all those distractions are killing our productivity. So turn off the email notifications, set your phone to silent, and hang a 'do not disturb' sign on your door.

If it's impossible to focus in your actual office, carve out time elsewhere each day, whether that's a coffee shop up the road, an unused conference room, or a janitor's closet where no one will think to look for you.

5. Stop multitasking

Multitasking is a myth. Scientific research has demonstrated that multitasking is actually switching rapidly between tasks and that it costs us time and energy each time we switch. So instead of doing two (or more) things at once, with the help of task management, tackle your to-do list one item at a time and don't move on until an item is completed.

6. Take breaks

While it may feel counterproductive to take breaks, studies show that taking breaks can increase productivity. Breaks are also good for your physical and mental health and can help re-energize you for the task at hand.

One exception is that when you're in a 'flow'– a state of effortless productivity– it's best not to interrupt yourself. Otherwise, go for a walk, grab a coffee, water your office plants, and then come back refreshed.

7. Have fewer meetings

Meetings are necessary for project management, and some of us actually like meetings. Weird, I know. However, having too many meetings can steal time from work on the project itself. And, let's be honest, our meetings far too often go long, get off-topic, and don't result in the answers we were hoping for.

Before scheduling or accepting a meeting, ask yourself whether its goals could be accomplished with an email or phone call, and do your best to avoid unnecessary meetings.

Do more in less time using productivity tools

Our whole discussion about productivity at work can be understood in terms of individual and team-building activities. Goal setting, prioritization, and personal schedule management are some project management skills anyone on your team can learn and implement on his own.

As the project manager, you have the ability to give your team additional productivity tools in the form of well-timed meetings, kanban boards, effective goal setting and monitoring, good project management software, and a healthy work environment.

Whether you're managing your first project or your thousandth, having an online project management software like Kissflow Project can help make these simple changes can increase productivity for you and your team.

FOUR

STOP DISTRACTING YOURSELF

Social media platforms bombast you with dopamine and information. As a result, when you sit to work, you can't concentrate.

Nonetheless, you can start to include boredom in your life. Hence you'll improve your attention span, as you won't bombast your brain with unimaginable amounts of data.

For instance, who will be more productive, a person on his phone or someone who just finished a 10 minutes meditation session?

Of course, the person that meditates will be more productive, as his brain is more transparent and less crowded with said distractions.

To summarize, you must stop distracting yourself with cheap entertainment. If you want to succeed in life and become more productive, you must minimize the amount of time you're distracted; instead, embrace boredom.

Easily Distracted? 11 Tips on How to Not Get Distracted

learning how to not get distracted is a tough goal to have. Most days, you sit at your desk, ready to finally get some work done. "Okay, lets do this," you think to yourself. You scroll over to Word or Google Drive and open up a fresh document. You have some idea of what needs to be done, but what happens next?

You write a few words down but just can't stay focused. Then you say, "Maybe I should wake myself up with something fun." You go to Facebook, 20 minutes gone. Then comes an hour of mindlessly watching a handful of YouTube videos. Before you know it, lunchtime has come, and half the day is gone.

If you're a typical working indian, you'll be distracted every 11 minutes; and, it will take you 25 minutes to settle down again to your task. Additionally, the more complicated your project, the longer it will take to regain your focus. This happens because your brain has to put in considerable effort when switching between complex objectives.

Distractions have a huge cost on our focus and productivity. If you want to improve or increase your focus, you need to learn to deal with the distractions in your life, and here's how.

1. Keep Your Vision and Goals in Mind

It's important to start with a good base for your focus as you learn how to avoid distraction. This means figuring out exactly why you need to focus in the first place. Do you have a big presentation at work next week that you need to prepare for? Do you have a dream of learning to play the guitar and need to focus for an hour each day while you practice?

Deciding what your ultimate goal is will help you dedicate yourself to learning how to focus. Knowing why we need to stay focused can help us push through the tough and tedious parts of accomplishing our goals. That's when our ability to focus is really tested and when it's most needed.

2. Clarify Your Day Before You Start

In the morning, before your workday begins, dedicate a few minutes to managing your schedule. A great way to do it is by applying the Covey time management matrix. Have a moment to set your priorities and determine which tasks are truly vital and urgent that day, which are not so urgent but still very important, and which you should avoid, either by delegating or eliminating them altogether.

This last type of task may be tricky because they will often be urgent, though uninspiring, issues, like questions from colleagues concerning their problems, phone calls, and emails that you answer by default, only because you've always done it and that's the way it's always been.

Instead, take control and make a conscious decision of what you're going to when they come knocking. Once you've made it, hold on to it, and ruthlessly follow through.

3. Reduce the Chaos of Your Day

If you have 20 tasks you need done every day, how effective do you think your focus ability will be?

You can't expect to do those things with sophistication if you're too scatterbrained to focus. You need to break it down to the essentials if you want to learn how to not get distracted.

Focus on only doing 2-3 important tasks a day, but no more than that. It's all you need to take steps towards accomplishing your goals. Slower is much better than giving up early because you took on too much, too soon. Ultimately, this is better for your mental health as you'll continuously see yourself moving forward without getting easily distracted.

4. Do Those Tasks as Soon as Possible

In order to make sure you get those 2 to 3 tasks done, you need to do them early in order to stay focused on the task without feeling overwhelmed. This means that as soon as you wake up, you're already plotting how to do them.

It's tough, but waiting to do them later only invites distraction to take over. Those distractions will inevitably come in the form of unexpected emails, social media, a child that needs your attention, or coworkers who need a helping hand on their projects. All of this can drain your willpower and make focusing on the task at hand much more difficult.

5. Focus on the Smallest Part of Your Work at a Time

An easy way to kill your focus is to see a goal for the big, giant accomplishment that it is. Most goals will at least take a few weeks to months to accomplish, and knowing that can make it feel like it'll take too long to do.

This will cause you to do one of two things:

You become discouraged because the goal is too big.

You fantasize about what it'll feel like to achieve the goal.

Either is terrible for your focus and always a potential problem when focusing on the big picture or using visualization.

Instead, focus on doing a very small, minimum amount of work.

For example, if you need to write an article, you know you'll need about 1000 words. If that seems like a lot, plan to write 200 words each day for the next five days (or adjust this according to the given deadline). Breaking it down like this will help the task feel more manageable, helping you learn how to not get distracted along the way.

6. Visualize Yourself Working

I briefly mentioned in tip 4 that visualization techniques can hurt you more than help you sometimes. However, there is a proper way of using visualization, and it's by visualizing yourself actually working.

Champion runners use this technique to great effect, usually by working backwards. They imagine themselves winning at first, and then they act out the whole process in reverse, feeling and visualizing each step all the way to the beginning.[1]

A quicker and more relevant way to apply this would be to imagine yourself doing a small part of the task at hand.

For instance, if you need to practice the guitar, but it's all the way across the room (let's assume maximum laziness for the sake of this example), what should you do?

First, imagine standing up (really, think of the sensation of getting up, and then do it). If you really imagined it, visualized and felt the act of standing up, then acting on that feeling will be easy.

Then, repeat the visualization process with each step till you have that guitar in hand and you're playing it. The process of focusing so intently on each step distracts you from how much you don't want to do something, and the visualizations ready your body for each step you need done.

All you need to do is apply this process to whatever it is you need to focus on.

7. Control Your Internal Distractions

Internal distractions are one of those problems you can't really run away from. You need to find ways to prepare your mind for work, and find simple ways to keep it from straying to non-essential thoughts in order to learn how to not get distracted.

There are a few types of internal distractions:

Priority Chaos

One of the most common distractions we encounter is that we have too many options on hand. This can cause priority chaos.

For example, some people may find it hard to focus at home because there are too many options to choose from. You can choose to feed your dog, read a book, watch TV, have a snack or take a nap.

Besides the costs of distraction mentioned before, priority chaos is a big demotivator. When there are too many potentially attractive options, it's hard to focus your energy and choose one of them – ideally the one you should be doing.

Priority chaos is also a demotivator because it makes you feel guilty. When you let your internal distractions overtake your focus, you're the one who chooses to divert your own attention and energy away from your task. So when the task you wanted to complete doesn't get done, you can't blame an external factor. Whether you do it consciously or not, you'll end up blaming yourself!

Why does priority chaos happen? Well, your brain subconsciously prioritizes tasks based on three factors:

To fulfil an existing need. For example, you need to go to the bathroom urgently, so your brain is guaranteed to prioritize it.

To achieve a certain feeling of satisfaction, such as the satisfaction of eating a delicious chocolate fudge cake.

The perceived cost of achieving the benefit. What is the effort, energy or time required to complete this action?

The brain automatically take these 3 factors into account even when you're not thinking about it.

Unfortunately, unless you're consciously making an effort, your brain is not always the best at making accurate judgement calls. It tends to have a bias towards short term benefits and short term costs.

As there are often many more options our brains link to short term benefits, when you're trying to focus on a task that gives you a long term benefit, that task usually becomes low priority. This is the essence of Priority Chaos.

Short & Long Term Mismatch

As explained earlier, our brains are not good at evaluating and comparing short term and long term benefits.

Short term benefits usually have a relatively low cost and are concrete, allowing our brains to easily grasp them.

We usually associate long term benefits with high cost, and these perceived costs are usually not as clear cut. The longer term it is, the more effort it takes to imagine the benefits. This automatically creates a mental barrier and resistance in our brains. As a result, we tend to trade long term gain for short term gains.

This is the reason why you might know that something is good for you in the long term, such as losing weight and exercising, but for some reason, you can't force yourself to feel excited about it. On the other hand, you might know that something is bad for you, such as binge eating junk food. But, the anticipation of short term satisfaction overwhelms your conscious ability to resist it.

This internal distraction is just like instant gratification. Thankfully, this can be tackled, too:

Identify what task needs the most focus to get accomplished.

Break down the tasks into smaller, bite-sized tasks. Each bite-sized task should have a very clear short term benefit (something that you can easily describe in one sentence), and a very clear short term cost (something that you can quantify, such as time spent).

Set a time limit or duration for each bite sized task. The time limit should be short enough so that it's a no-brainer to want to check it off.

Evaluate your other options. Be realistic about what they are! Write them all down, and list out the benefits and the costs associated.

Once you have your list completed, start prioritizing them. You have a time limit, so you need to order your tasks by priority, starting with the focus task as your top priority. Then fit the others around it.

Schedule the remaining tasks for another time. For any remaining tasks on the list that won't fit within your allocated time, don't worry. You don't have to give them up. Just schedule them for another time.

8. Remove External Distractions

This tip is a bit more straightforward as it requires you to simply distance yourself physically from things that are causing distractions.

If the television is disrupting, turn it off or work in another room. If your kids are playing and yelling, try getting up to work before they wake up. If you keep checking your phone, put your phone on silent while you're working. Empty the wall in front of you to keep your mind on track. Photos, prints and various knick-knacks you like to display may be cute, but they will make your mind wander.

It's usually obvious what you should do, but you still shouldn't overlook this piece of advice.

9. Skip What You Don't Know

This is a tip I don't see often enough. If you hit a snag in your work, then come back to it later as you learn how to not get distracted. Focus your attention on what you can do to keep working "mindlessly" at all costs. All this means is that you should focus on the easy parts first.

Eventually, you can come back to the more difficult parts, and hopefully by then it'll have come to you or you'll have built up enough momentum that it won't break your focus if you work on it.

10. Improve Your Discipline With Focus Practice

There are a few focus exercises you can do to improve your overall discipline.

The first one is meditation, which is basically the definition of focus in practice. It's a great method for building focus ability, de-stressing, and giving you greater control over your emotions.

The second exercise is the Pomodoro method, which asks you to set a timer to track the time you spend on a task. These are basically "focus sprints," and each one is followed by a solid break. Like real sprints, you'll get better and better at doing them over time. Each interval improves your ability to stay focused when it matters, helping you learn how to not get distracted in the long term.

11. Manage Your Momentum

Momentum is like a discipline lubricant–it helps ease the process of sticking with goals. That's why I think it's important that we never take true breaks from our goals; we end up losing momentum and relying on discipline to get back on track (not an easy thing to do).

This means each and every day, we need to do something significant to further our goals (yes, even weekends and holidays). And when I say "significant," I don't necessarily mean a big task, but rather, any task that brings us closer to our goals.

For instance, if your goal is to be a freelance writer, then write one single pitch on a weekend. If your goal is to get healthy, then go for a short, 5-minute walk, even on Christmas day.

The Bottom Line

Learning how to not get distracted is certainly easier said than done. Distractions exist in every corner of our lives these days, even if it's in the form of a short beep generated from a notification. These kinds of distractions can seem minimal, but anything that pulls you away from your focus can get in the way of your productivity.

Don't get distracted. Instead, use some of the tips above to win back your focus and overcome distractions.

FIVE

HOW TO USE MEDITATION TO IMPROVE PRODUCTIVITY

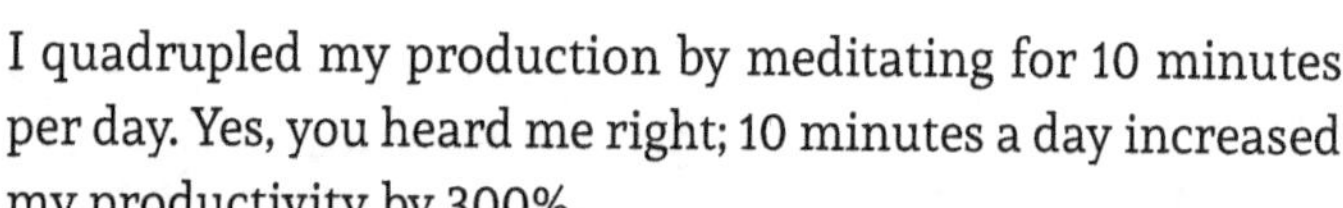

I quadrupled my production by meditating for 10 minutes per day. Yes, you heard me right; 10 minutes a day increased my productivity by 300%.

So, if you desire to be more productive, meditation may be what you lack in life, and that's for a single reason; it improves your focus.

Today, we can't help but be distracted by infinite sources, primarily social media. Because of that, we habitually jump from one piece of information to another without noticing it!

Hence when you sit down to work, which is a low-stimulus activity, your brain will reject it.

Honestly, I don't see myself not meditating for a single day, as it has helped me to achieve the freedom to work and be as productive as I want.

Meditation — a valuable yet unappreciated asset

Few are the people that genuinely appreciate meditation for what it is.

Today's world is filled with countless distractions. As a result, our ability to focus decreases. In fact, the more distracted we are, the less our attention span will be.

For instance, if you constantly scroll on social media, your brain will get accustomed to jumping from one task to another.

However, meditation has the opposite effect of social media and all distractions; it allows you to be undistracted for extended periods.

I don't see how people wouldn't want a tad bit of peace in their lives. Medical publications have repeatedly proved both the short- and long-term benefits of meditation.

So, how can I start to meditate?

Simple. To meditate, close your eyes and focus on your breath. Then, naturally, your mind will begin to wander. Return to the present and focus on your breath again when it happens. Do it for as long as you want to.

Meditation is an excellent fit for just that if you want to become more focused and thus more productive.

Next, let's examine the correlation between meditation and productivity.

The correlation between meditation and productivity

The more you involve yourself with cheap entertainment, the less productive you'll be in the long term.

Because of that, every book about productivity will suggest deleting all social media accounts, as it's the most potent source.

However, you don't have to take such a drastic step so quickly; for now, stick to minimizing or lowering the amount of time you spend distracted.

A suitable platform to eliminate or minimize distractions- is, you guessed it, meditation.

When you meditate, you're undistracted. As such, you habituate sitting down and doing the tedious work, which is frequently the one that leads to most of the results.

The more you meditate, the better your attention span will get. As a result, you're more likely to sit and be in a state of depth (deep work). Thus, you'll produce more work in less time.

How Meditation Can Help to Improve Your Productivity

As business competition is rising tremendously, being innovative and productive is the best choice for employees who want to retain their jobs. Employees who work hard and devote more and more time to being productive end up becoming very stressed. Stressful minds will never be productive and in most case, the employee will start hating their job. You can improve your productivity when your mind is at peace and that will only occur with tools like meditation and yoga. Meditation is a state of mind where you think about nothing. It has historical value and is considered to be a gateway of cosmic energy. It provides clarity in thoughts that result in a tension-free and blissful life.

Meditation is a simple, effective method that can help you to improve your productivity. If you are completely relaxed and stress-free, then your mind will also work more effectively. The right side of our brain, which is responsible for creating new ideas, will work actively when you do meditation regularly. As a result, you will be able to produce new designs and ideas for your business. It might sound bizarre that you can improve your productivity just by sitting quietly and alone, but it's true. The most surprising fact is that this short time will improve your entire day. So, regularly invest some time into meditation so that you can gain some fruitful results in return. Meditation has great soothing as well as relaxing effects. Lets us discuss some of the important benefits of Meditation.

As business competition is rising tremendously, being innovative and productive is the best choice for employees who want to retain their jobs. Employees who work hard and devote more and more time to being productive end up becoming very stressed. Stressful minds will never be productive and in most case, the employee will start hating their job. You can improve your productivity when your mind is at peace and that will only occur with tools like meditation and yoga. Meditation is a state of mind where you think about nothing. It has historical value and is considered to be a gateway of cosmic energy. It provides clarity in thoughts that result in a tension-free and blissful life.

Meditation is a simple, effective method that can help you to improve your productivity. If you are completely relaxed and stress-free, then your mind will also work more effectively. The right side of our brain, which is responsible for creating new ideas, will work actively when you do meditation regularly. As a result, you will be able to produce new designs and ideas for your business. It might sound bizarre that you can improve your productivity just by sitting quietly and alone, but it's true. The most surprising fact is that this short time will improve your entire day. So, regularly invest some time into meditation so that you can gain some fruitful results in return. Meditation has great soothing as well as relaxing effects. Lets us discuss some of the important benefits of Meditation.

SIX
MINDSET

The Science Behind Your Head and What It Means for Your Productivity, Happiness and Success

Introduction

What is a Mindset?

A mindset is a set of beliefs that influences the way we live, work and think. A mindset can be influenced by many different factors such as our culture, education, experience etc. In this article we will explore various mindset theories and their definitions.

The definition of a mindset is an area of study in psychology that refers to attitudes or beliefs about oneself, the future or aspects of the world around us. The term comes from the ancient Greek word 'mindset' which means 'the positioning of a system before consideration' (Liddell et al.). To put it simply, it is how we see ourselves or how we think about life in general.

Mindset theories in psychology are not necessarily concerned with what may be going on inside someone's head — thoughts

—

in psychology and other fields, the term 'mindset' is used to refer to a group of beliefs that one has about their capabilities, aptitudes and intelligence.

The term "mindset" can be used to describe both a) a general orientation or outlook on life, usually psychological or sociological in nature, b) the tendency for people within a certain culture or organization to have common ways of thinking about things.

The word "mindset" was coined by Richard Beckhard and Donald Clifton in 1975 in their work on how people's attitudes towards what they can accomplish influence how they do. The concept of mindset was developed further by Carol Dweck in her book Mindset: The New Psychology of Success (2006).

—

A mindset is the mental attitude with which one approaches a given situation. It is quite similar to a personality, but it usually has more of an indirect influence on people's actions.

The idea of a mindset was brought about by Carol Dweck, who published her first book about mindsets in 2006. Her research and ideas have evolved over the years and she has published other books to explore mindsets even further.

Some examples of different mindsets are: growth mindset and fixed mindset, high-power and low-power mindset, self-fulfilling prophecy mindset and fixed self-concept belief system.

The Impact of Mindset in the Workplace

—

Our work environment deeply impacts our mental health.

The workplace usually has a negative impact on one's mental health. Sixty-two percent of U.S. employees report feeling tired, sluggish, or otherwise mentally drained frequently from the time they spend at their jobs. A whopping seventeen percent of U.S. workers say that they "never" have time for themselves outside of work because they are always focused on their job responsibilities, and this can be detrimental to one's well being.

How to Improve your Mindset for Increased Productivity & Limitless Happiness

It is a well-known fact that a happy and confident mindset can lead to an increase in productivity.

However, the other side of this theory is that not being confident can lead to decreased productivity.

This article will explore some techniques on how you can improve your mindset for increased productivity and limitless happiness.

Remember that one of the key ingredients to increased happiness is self-confidence. And with a positive outlook, you're more likely to see the opportunities in your life instead of the obstacles or barriers.

The first thing you should do before trying any other technique is take five minutes to meditate or spend time alone and reflect on how wonderful life really is.

—

"The most powerful weapon on earth is the human soul on fire." — Napoleon Bonaparte

A person's mental health is an all-important factor in terms of productivity, decision-making and happiness. Confidence boosting quotes and positivity quotes generator can help you improve your mindset and feel happier within minutes.

SEVEN
UN MOTIVATION

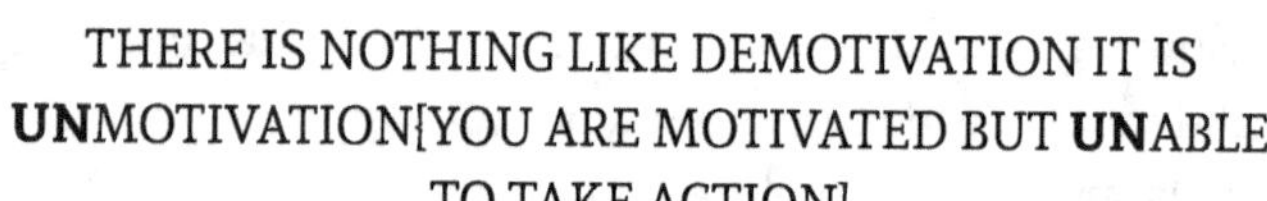

1.Understand why you feel unmotivated

If you're feeling unmotivated, it's important to understand why. Usually, there are one or more underlying reasons for why you feel this way. Once you identify the cause of your unmotivation, you can start to take steps to address it. In this blog post, we'll explore some of the most common reasons why people feel unmotivated and what you can do about it.

to workout One reason you might feel unmotivated to work out is because you don't have a specific goal in mind. Working out without a goal is like driving without a destination. It's hard to stay motivated if you're not sure why you're doing something. Another reason you might feel unmotivated to work out is because you don't enjoy it. If working out feels like a chore, it's no wonder you don't want to do it. Try finding an activity that is both challenging and enjoyable, such as hiking, biking, or swimming. Finally, make sure you are giving yourself enough time to rest and recover between workouts. fatigue can lead to a lack of motivation.

2.Find something that excites you

A new book, a new project, a new idea.

You've just hit upon a grand new project or ambitious new book idea, and now the planning begins in earnest. This is an exciting time, when everything feels possible and you can't wait to get started. But it's also a time when it's important to be realistic and make sure you're setting yourself up for success. First, take a step back and consider what your goals are for this project. Are you hoping to write a bestseller? Make a profit? Reach a certain audience? Once you know what you want to achieve, you can start mapping out a plan to make it happen. Next, think about what resources you have available to make your project a success. Do you have the time, money, and skill set necessary to complete it? If not, what can you realistically do to acquire these things? Finally, consider your timeline. When do you hope to have this project finished? What milestones do you need to hit along the way? Make sure your timeline is achievable; otherwise, you'll likely end up feeling frustrated and discouraged.

3.Set small, achievable goals

that keep you going Keep track of milestones Give yourself rewards (for example, a treat)Focus on self-compassion (instead of self-criticism)Challenge negative beliefs Set boundaries with other people Find your support community Remember: If you feel like you're putting too much pressure on yourself to meet self-care goals, it can do more harm than good.(3) Stick With Your Self-Care Plan No matter how motivated or inspired we are to take care of ourselves, some days are just harder than others. Factors that can make it tough to stick with your plan include stressful work deadlines, bad traffic and daily life challenges. When these things happen, it isn't always possible to give yourself the time and attention that you would like. When this happens don't try and be perfect. Be kinder to yourself by being flexible in giving back to a healthy lifestyle by following a sound nutrition plan according to Meta Day

4. Make a plan

Make a plan to stay organized and productive. Next, choose a productivity strategy to help you stay on track. Popular strategies include: Schedule appointments with yourself. Block off time in your calendar to regularly de-clutter and organize. If you don't schedule time to do this, it won't happen. Take time to purge old papers you don't need, supplies you no longer use and to weed out old files. Consider biting off a small area to organize in just 30 minutes. Make this a weekly habit and you'll tackle all sorts of areas in your office and home. Likewise, block off and protect chunks of time on your calendar for high priority activities. If you know there's something you want to get done in a given day, make an appointment with yourself and then honor that time (meaning when the appointment rolls around, work on that task or project). Seeing the appointment visibly can also make it easier to say "no" to something or someone else that might serve as a barrier to your productivity on the priority.

Keep your long-term goals in mind and think about the ways you can achieve them. Keep your long-term goals in mind and think about the ways you can achieve them. Prioritize your workload by scheduling the most important tasks first. Make daily, weekly and monthly to-do lists of important tasks. Review your daily priorities at the beginning of each day.

5. Get rid of distractions

How to reduce distractions and focus on work. Don't get distracted. Instead, use some of the tips above to win back your focus and overcome distractions. Your productivity will thank you. Begin building habits that help you eliminate distractions and stay focused. Start by creating an environment in which you're less tempted to get preoccupied with something other than what you're working on. This isn't always easy to do. For one, many of us rely on a computer to do our work, but we also find our biggest distractions enabled by the use of a computer on the internet. If you constantly find yourself wandering over to video or shopping websites, try using a website blocker app.

In short, be mindful of your thoughts, instead of allowing yourself to skip between task and distraction. Remove as many excuses and distractions as you can so you can bring your full attention to one task at a time — no multitasking. To eliminate distractions, give yourself a shorter time frame to finish your work. This is like giving yourself an artificial deadline, but backed up with something that holds you accountable. Tell your boss or client that you'll give them a draft of a project by the end of the day. Find an accountability partner who will hold you to your target time frame. However you do it, setting a hard deadline will help you avoid distractions and amp up your productivity.

Internal distractions are one of those problems you can't really run away from. You need to find ways to prepare your mind for work, and find simple ways to keep it from straying to non-essential thoughts in order to learn how to not get distracted. Try to adopt new habits to help you to control your distractors. Carefully assess your phone, messaging and email usage, and limit the time that you spend on social media.

Final Words

When you're distracted, your ability to focus lowers. In fact, the more you indulge yourself in cheap entertainment, the less productive you'll be.

If you want to improve your productivity, you must let go of all distractions; for most people, that'll be to cease the use of social media.

you can follow me on instagram @aviral_pathak_ or mail us at *unlitework@gmail.com*

9 798888 722795